BY THE SAME AUTHOR:-

PUSS IN BOOTS

FIRST PUBLISHED 1983

Reprinted 1985
ⓒ Caroline Bennitt

ISBN 0 907926 10 X

CHARACTERS

SANTA - rosy-cheeked, plump, traditional Father Christmas
RUDOLPH - reindeer with antlers and remarkable nose
QUEEN - of Snow and Ice, bossy, haughty and white-robed

BADDIES
GIANT - huge, foolish, humourless (Jack & the Beanstalk)
SILVER - Long John, vicious, one-legged pirate with parrot
SCROOGE - nightgowned, nightcapped, sullen miser
UGLY 1 - tall, thin, alcoholic dame (Cinderella)
UGLY 2 - stoutly buxom, voluptuous dame (Cinderella)

GOODIES
CINDERS - rag-clad but happy Cinderella
ALADDIN - scantily clad, oriental principal boy
PUSS - in Boots, fashion-conscious, confident feline
ROBIN - Hood, swash-buckling outlaw principal boy
GOOSE - Mother, over-dressed, theatrical camp dame

TOYS
SPACE - the latest in astronauts
COPPER - old-fashioned, on-beat policeman
NURSE - efficient Red Cross worker
DOLL - golden-haired dancer
TEDDY - furry, brown and cuddly

SUGGESTED EXTRAS
WITCH, DEMON KING; GOLDILOCKS, RED RIDING-HOOD; DUCK, SOLDIER, SAILOR, BALLERINA, NATIONAL DRESS DOLLS, JACK-IN-THE-BOX.

THE ACTION TAKES PLACE AT THE NORTH POLE ON CHRISTMAS EVE. IT IS SNOWING. RUDOLPH SLEEPS BESIDE THE SLEIGH. ENTER SANTA.

SANTA: Wake up Rudolph, you dozy old deer.
You can't be sleepy - you've slept a whole year.
Come along, rise and shine. Christmas is here.

RUDOLPH RISES RELUCTANTLY. WIND AND SNOW GROW STRONGER.

SANTA: Now be a good fellow and light your nose.
My fingers are freezing and so are my toes.
But still, it's more Christmassy when it snows.

RUDOLPH'S NOSE GLOWS. SNOW SWIRLS. ENTER QUEEN.

SANTA: And here comes the Queen of Snow and Ice.
             Jolly good, Queeny. It's twice as nice
             When Christmas is white.

QUEEN: Take my advice
             And stop all that hearty merriment stuff:
             It's putting me in the most frightful huff.
             This nonsense has gone on long enough.

SANTA: Poor old Snow Queen. But not to worry.
             No need to get into such a flurry.
             Come along, Rudolph. We'll have to hurry.

QUEEN STOPS HIM WITH AN ACCUSING LONG POINTED FINGER.

MUSIC 1:   "HARK THE HERALD ANGELS SING"

QUEEN: Hark to me, and what I sing:
             You're a rotten Winter king.
             Winter should be cold and freezing –
             Everybody sad and sneezing.

             You make Winter glad and bright.
             I can't stand it so, tonight
             Winter shall return to frost:
             Christmas Day shall now be lost.

             Hark to me, and what I say:
             I abolish Christmas Day!

MUSIC ENDS. SANTA APPLAUDS, THINKING SHE IS JOKING.

SANTA: Still, Christmas is what the world enjoys,
             So now I must go and load the toys
             To cheer all the little girls and boys.
             So long, lovely, we have to go.
             Thanks for all the scenic snow.
             And nobody else hates Christmas, you know.

QUEEN: Oh yes they do.
SANTA: Oh no they don't.
QUEEN: Oh yes they DO!
SANTA: Oh no they DON'T!

QUEEN: You are mistaken. Wait and see.
             Plenty of people agree with me.

MUSIC 2: "O COME, ALL YE FAITHFUL"

QUEEN: O come, all you baddies,
             Come and cancel Christmas,
             O come, help me stop this dreadful
             Frolicsome rot.
             End all rejoicing.
             Let's get rid of Santa.

BADDIES START ENTERING

QUEEN: O come, you all abhor him.

BADDIES: We come, we all abhor him.
We come, we all abhor him
And hate all this lot.

MUSIC ENDS. BUSINESS WITH AUDIENCE WHO BOO AND HISS.

SANTA: But how can YOU hate Christmas Time?
You all star in Pantomime.

BADDIES: Yes, but what makes us all mad, is:
Everybody boos the Baddies.

AUDIENCE BOOS.

BADDIES: See?

SANTA: But you're famous. You're all great. You
Can't believe they REALLY hate you.
It's just fun, so why the fuss?

GIANT: 'Cos it ISN'T fun for us!

MUSIC 3: "ONCE IN ROYAL DAVID'S CITY"

GIANT: Once I was a happy Giant,
Living high above the clouds.
Now because of Jack and his Beanstalk
I get booed at by the crowds.
Loose my grip, and lose my head.
How they cheer, to see me dead.

Jack comes up, from Earth to my place,
Fools my wife, to let him stay;
Steals my hen, that lays the golden eggs, and
Takes my harp and money away;
Hacks that beanstalk, till I fall.
If you're me, it isn't fun at all.

MUSIC ENDS. BADDIES SYMPATHISE.

SANTA: Oh, look here, be more sensible will you?
Clearly Jack doesn't REALLY kill you -
Otherwise you couldn't be here ...

GIANT DOES NOT UNDERSTAND. SANTA INDICATES SILVER.

SANTA: Together with this fine buccaneer.

SANTA BOWS APPRECIATIVELY. SILVER IS IMMUNE TO FLATTERY.

SILVER: A buccaneer! Well, stap me vitals!
Shiver me timbers! Give me titles

6

Would you? you slimy mound of blubber!
You stinking whale of plump land-lubber.

SANTA IS ASTONISHED.

SILVER: Oh! For a grab o' me cat o' nine tails!
I'd soon whip the wind from yer fine sails!
Don't go smarming and trying to squire it:
Long John Silver's a PLAIN MEAN PIRATE.

MUSIC 4: "IT CAME UPON THE MIDNIGHT CLEAR"

SILVER: It came upon me, in a flash
Of icy, blinding white.
That a poor plain pirate I must stay
No matter how hard I fight.

My crew will always be revolt-
ing, I shall always lose.
I'll never grow another leg -
Would you be in my shoes?

MUSIC CONTINUES OVER DIALOGUE. SILVER SPEAKS PARROT.

SILVER: I mean shoe.
PARROT: Shoo yourself!
SILVER: Boot, then.
PARROT: Put the boot in! Put the boot in!
SILVER: I'm singing a song. Put a sock in it, will you?
PARROT: Sock it to me. Sock it to me.
SILVER: Now, where was I?

MUSIC SWELLS.

SILVER: The schooner Hispaniola sails
To Treasure Island far,
With Squire Trelawney, Doctor Live-
sey, And Aah Jim Lad, the star.

I nearly fools them, every time
But every time I'm twigged.
If you ask me, it's a pantomime -
And I'm starting to think it's rigged.

MUSIC ENDS.

SANTA: But of course it is. And you help to unfold it -
Just as R. L. Stevenson told it.

SILVER: Then what's the POINT? I worrits and schemes,
And plots me plans, and dreams me dreams,
But: Yo ho ho, and a bottle of rum
And - hang me! I've forgotten Ben Gunn!
I NEVER remember! And ...

PARROT: Pieces of Eight!

SILVER: And that's another thing I hate:
              Getting stuck with this dimwit Polly
              And NEVER getting me hands on the lolly.
              It isn't FAIR!

SCROOGE: Of course it ain't.
              And I've got an even worse complaint.

MUSIC 5:   "THE FIRST NOWELL"

              The first of the ghosts
Is as merry as they come.
But the second one is gloomy,
And the third's downright glum.
They fill me full of guilt,
And they empty my purse.
It's the Dickens of a predicament,
And it keeps getting worse.
No thank you, no more. Merry Christmas? No fear.
It's a humbug, it's a bore, and I've had it up to here.

How would YOU like to be Scrooge?
Getting dragged out of bed,
In this silly frilly nightie,
With a bobble on your head?
Being made to give your cash
To the Cratchit family?
All the world weeps for Tiny Tim
But no-one thinks of me!

No more presents, no more games. No more food, no more fun.
I say "Humbug" to Christmas, "Ya Boo!" to everyone.

MUSIC ENDS. BUSINESS WITH AUDIENCE.

SANTA: But Scrooge, they love you when you turn good,
         And send that turkey and Christmas pud.

SCROOGE: But I don't LIKE being good; it's nicer
         To stay as I am: a crotchety miser.

SANTA: I don't believe you. Nor do I believe
         These two lovely creatures have cause to grieve.

SANTA INDICATES UGLIES. UGLIES FLOUNCE.

UGLY 1: Fat lot you care for our bleeding hearts!

UGLY 2: And the PANGS we suffer, when Christmas starts.

MUSIC 6: "WE THREE KINGS"

              Two enchanting sisters are we.
Dressed to kill, and striking to see.

UGLY 1: Tall and slender
UGLY 2: Sweet and tender
BOTH: No-one could disagree,
          BUT
          Every Christmas makes us wince.
          Though we prance, and strut, and mince,
          Everyone boos us, nobody woos us,
          Sister Cinders gets the Prince.

UGLY 1: I'm as slim as one could desire.
UGLY 2: I'm more plump, with more to admire.
UGLY 1: I'm available,
UGLY 2: I'm assailable,
BOTH: Why aren't the men on fire?
          BECAUSE
          Every Christmas it's the same.
          You give us an Ugly name.
          Everyone hisses us, nobody kisses us,
          Nobody fancies a Pantomime Dame.

MUSIC ENDS. UGLIES WEEP AND SNIFF. UGLY 1 PRODUCES HIP-FLASK.

UGLY 1: All those boos have driven me to booze. (SWIGS)

SANTA: But they adore you.

UGLY 2:   Which one would YOU choose?
          She's got the booze, but I've got all the boosom.
          (THRUSTING HER CHEST AT HIM)

SANTA: You're both just ... grand. A truly lovely twosome.

UGLY 2: You truly lying swine! We're both just gruesome.
          We're fed up with flattering false adoration.

UGLY 1: So that's why we've come at the Queen's invitation.

GIANT: I'm not putting up with no more aggravation.

SILVER: Me fingers are itching for retaliation.

UGLY 1: I've suffered too much. Oh! The humiliation!

UGLY 2: The sheer degradation! The infuriation!

SANTA: But, Baddies, you're part of the great celebration,
          The jubilant, Christmassy jollification.
          If you go on strike, it will cause consternation.

QUEEN: We're not merely striking. For your information
          We're here to cause Christmas's extermination!

MUSIC 7: "GOD REST YOU MERRY, GENTLEMEN"

BADDIES: So rot your Merry Christmassing
          And down with Pantomimes.

We've had enough of people hissing
At our wicked crimes.
We're off to find the fun we're missing -
Roll on evil times.
OH!
Tidings of misery and gloom,
Trouble and doom,
Oh, tidings of misery and gloom.

There's nothing you can do, we're going to
Have our wicked way.
There's nothing in the world we hate as
Much as Christmas Day.
We really will be cheerful, when we
Hear the people say:
"OH!
Tidings of misery and gloom,.
Trouble and doom,
Oh, tidings of misery and gloom."

MUSIC ENDS. BADDIES CHUCKLE, CACKLE AND TAUNT AUDIENCE.

QUEEN: Stop gloating for a moment, Baddies, please!
It's not enough that Santa's on his knees.
To foil him, we must put him in deep freeze.
So, stand and stop him, if he tries evasion,
While I intone my strongest incantation.
And NOBODY disturb my concentration.

BADDIES FORM SEMI-CIRCLE ROUND SANTA. QUEEN STARTS MAGIC.

MUSIC 8: "IN THE BLEAK MIDWINTER"

QUEEN: In the bleak midwinter
Frosty winds make moan;
Earth stands hard as iron,
Water like a stone.
Rosy cheeks and laughing lips
Have no part to play.
So, may aching numbness
Steal all joys away.

Icy flowers of crystal
Creep along your veins,
Whitely cling together
In their frozen chains.
Motionless, a snowman now
Powerless remain.
Never shall bleak winter
Laugh or smile again.

MUSIC ENDS. BADDIES TAP SANTA, WHO IS NOW HARD-FROZEN.

SCROOGE: Oh, well done, Snow Queen. Solid as a rock.

SILVER: He's clapped in irons nothing can unlock.

GIANT: Now I don't have to be a laughing-stock.

UGLY 2: And people won't be rude about my frock.

UGLY 1: No audiences now will flock to mock.

SCROOGE: (PEERING AT AUDIENCE BY LIGHT OF HIS LANTERN)
THIS audience is in a state of shock.

SILVER: (LEERING AT AUDIENCE THROUGH HIS TELESCOPE)
Ha ha, me hearties. Scuppered are you, eh?

QUEEN: Now come along. Put Santa on his sleigh
And tow the nasty vulgar thing away.

BADDIES LIFT SANTA ONTO SLEIGH AND TOW IT OFF, SINGING

MUSIC 9: "WE WISH YOU A MERRY CHRISTMAS"

BADDIES: We wish you a horrid Christmas,
We wish you a lousy Christmas,
We wish you a mouldy Christmas
And a nasty New Year.

Bad tidings we bring,
And that's why we sing:
We wish you a smelly Christmas
(SPOKEN) And a perfectly ghastly New Year.

BADDIES RETURN WITH THINGS TO THROW AT THE AUDIENCE. MUSIC.

BADDIES: We wish you a rotten Christmas,
We wish you a beastly Christmas,
We wish you a filthy Christmas
And a hateful New Year.

Bad tidings we bring,
And that's why we sing:
We wish you a dreadful Christmas
(SPOKEN) And an absolutely horribly AWFUL New Year!

BADDIES LEAVE, DODGING THINGS THROWN BACK BY AUDIENCE.
RUDOLPH IS LEFT ALONE AND WORRIED.

INTERLUDE

RUDOLPH: (TO AUDIENCE)
Oh dear me, this is terrible,
Whatever shall I do?
There's going to be no Christmas Day -
I can't believe it's true.
if only I could warn someone.
The problem, though, is who?
For nobody can hear me speak -
Except, of course, for you.

MUSIC 10:"WHAT CHILD IS THIS"/GREENSLEEVES

RUDOLPH: Now Rudolph is a red-eyed reindeer,
        Vainly trying not to sob.
        For no-one else, in the whole wide world, can
        Do poor Santa Claus's job.

        Dolls, games and cuddly toys are
        Sitting, waiting in the store.
        But only old Santa Claus knows
        Which toy a child will be waiting for.

        Oh, I could load the sleigh, and lead it
        Through the starry skies to glide.
        But I could never get down a chimney, with
        Antlers that stick out on either side.

        Rudolph is a red-eyed reindeer, and
        Now, to add to all my woes,
        I haven't got a hanky, and
        I really do need to blow my nose.

MUSIC ENDS. BUSINESS WITH AUDIENCE BORROWING HANKY.

ACT TWO

TINKLY MUSIC. THE TOYS ARE SITTING IN THE STORE.
CINDERS CREEPS IN, ADMIRING THE DECORATIONS AND TOYS.

CINDERS: How strange. I think my watch must be fast
        I thought it was Christmas Day at last,
        But no. The toys are still here, waiting.
        Silly me, I'm anticipating.
        Lovely Teddy Bear. How do you do? (SHAKES ITS PAW)
        I just can't WAIT for Christmas, can you?

MUSIC 11: "ON CHRISTMAS NIGHT ALL CHRISTIANS SING"

CINDERS: On Christmas Night it's ever such fun,
        For then I'm no longer the lonely one.
        A pumpkin, rats, mice, lizards - they're all
        Transformed to carry me to the ball.
        I get a fabulous glittering gown.
        And the Prince seeks me all over town.

        I don't mind having to slave in the muck,
        'Cos Fairy Godmother brings me luck.
        On Christmas Night, the Prince and I dance,
        And I drop my slipper - as if by chance.
        Oh, how I dread that Midnight Chime!
        Till then, I have a wonderful time.

CINDERS: All year I work as a scullery maid,
But I don't care that my joy's delayed.
On Christmas Night the tables are turned -
And all agree that my joy's well-earned.
When every lady my slipper has tried,
It fits me. I'm the Prince's bride.

I wish my Ugly Sisters could be
A tiny weeny bit kind to me.
I wish my father wasn't so broke,
But still, he's not such a bad old bloke.
I've really got no cause to complain,
Now that Christmas is here again.

MUSIC ENDS. CINDERS IS VERY PUZZLED.

CINDERS: Well, surely, it must be Christmas by now -
Unless I've muddled the dates somehow.
Let's see now, "Thirty days hath ... November?
April, and ..." bother! I never remember.
Perhaps it's a leap year or something; if so,
Then "February ..." but Aladdin will know.
Hello there, Aladdin. What IS going on?
I thought it was Christmas. Have I got it wrong?

ALADDIN COMES IN, ALSO PUZZLED.

ALADDIN: I wouldn't have thought so. Unless I have too.
I reckon that Christmas is just about due.
I'm longing to get all the merriment started.

RUDOLPH SHAKES HEAD, DROOPS TAIL, AND FAINTLY FLASHES NOSE.

CINDERS: But look at poor Rudolph. He seems downhearted.
His nose is ever so faint and pale.
And see how sadly he droops his tail.

ALADDIN: Poor old reindeer. Don't look so glum -
It's Christmas! Santa's soon bound to come.

RUDOLPH: (TO AUDIENCE)
If only I could communicate,
And let them know, before it's too late.

ALADDIN: I don't see how anything CAN be wrong -
Except our watches. I'll sing you a song.

MUSIC 12: "AS WITH GLADNESS MEN OF OLD" - Chinese style

ALADDIN: As with gladness I prepare,
Curl my shoes, and plait my hair,
Turn my eyes to narrow slits,
See my satin costume fits.
I can't wait for haunted caves.
Precious gems, and genii slaves.

Life in a laundry isn't posh,
But it comes out in the wash.
Painted pagodas, silk brocades,
Great receptions, grand parades.
Oriental splendour swells
All around with gongs and bells.

Though I face hair-raising trials,
I foil Abanazar's wiles.
Though as a fake lamp-trafficker
He whisks us to Africa.
Still, despite his wangles grim
Old Ma Twankey mangles him!

MUSIC ENDS.

CINDERS: I'm not surprised you're longing to get going.
I must admit my restlessness is growing.

ALADDIN: If Father Christmas would arrive, we could.

CINDERS: Is this him now? Oh no, it's Robin Hood.

ROBIN STRIDES IN VIGOROUSLY.

ROBIN: Hullo, has anyone seen Santa Claus?
And what are you two doing in his stores?

ALADDIN: We're looking for him too. It's getting serious.

CINDERS: His disappearance really is mysterious.

ROBIN: Well, not to worry. That would be unwise.

RUDOLPH FLASHES NOSE DESPERATELY, BUT NO-ONE NOTICES.

ROBIN: Perhaps he's planning some sort of surprise.

RUDOLPH: (TO AUDIENCE)
They're still convinced that Santa Claus will come.
How can I tell them? Why must I be dumb?
They should be planning some sort of attack
To make the Baddies give us Christmas back.
I flash my nose, but that they just ignore.
If only I knew Morse, or Semaphore.

ROBIN: Look, even Rudolph's nose is getting restive.
This hanging round is hardly very festive.
I should be out there, riding through the glen,
Rescuing Babes, and robbing wealthy men.

MUSIC 13: "DING DONG MERRILY ON HIGH" + "ANGELS FROM THE REALMS"

ROBIN: Zing bong, merrily I shoot.
I've never missed my mark yet.
Zing bong, every shot I shoot

Lands slap bang, right on target.
(SLAPS THIGH IN A SWASHBUCKLING WAY)

Friar Tuck and Little John, and all my Merry
Men, are waiting round the camp-fire,
Keen to do their duty;
Through Sherwood as we ride,
Our longbows by our side
The villains try to hide,
But
We still grab their booty.

Zing bong, merrily the lute
Of Allan-a-Dale is ringing.
On my horn I toot a hoot,
And out leap outlaws springing.

Maid Marion, and Richard Coeur-de-Lion,
Will Scarlet, and the others
Wait to start the fighting.
We never kill for kicks,
We get out of a fix
By playing clever tricks
It's
Ever so exciting.

Zing bong, what a super suit
Of Lincoln green and leather!
I look beautifully cute,
And manly, both together.

Prince John, and my Lord Bishop of Hereford, the
Sheriff of Nottingham, and
All my foes
Hate me something frightful.
They'd all like me deceased,
I don't mind in the least,
On venison I feast
My
Life is quite delightful.

MUSIC ENDS.

ROBIN: But all the same, there's not much satisfaction
Just singing of it. What I want is action.

ALADDIN: We all agree on that. But what's the use?

CINDERS: Is this him now? Oh no, it's Puss in Boots.

ENTER PUSS, SWEEPING LOW BOW WITH PLUMED HAT.

PUSS: My greetings, fellow principals. What news?
Is Santa Claus indulging in a snooze?
Or has he set off on a pleasure cruise?
Should some one fetch him? There's no time to lose.

ALADDIN: We've COME to fetch him, Puss; but he's not here.

ROBIN: No sign of Christmas anywhere, we fear

CINDERS: We can't think what has made him disappear.
         He'd hardly leave, with Christmas Day so near.

PUSS: You've found no note, no sign, no hint, no clue?

CINDERS: No, Puss. We're baffled, just as much as you.

PUSS: I'm never baffled. I'll know what to do.

ALADDIN: You will?

PUSS: Of course. Just ... let me think it through.

CINDERS: Oh good.

ROBIN: We need to act. Do something forceful.

ALADDIN: Well, come on Puss. You say you're so resourceful.

MUSIC 14: "DECK THE HALL WITH BOUGHS OF HOLLY"

PUSS: Let me now be wise and witty -
         Have a little think about our plight.
         Banish any sad self-pity,
         Organise a plan, to put things right.
         I'm a cunning, clever kitty,
         Winning all battles without a fight.
         I'm not merely rather pretty -
         I am rather more than pretty bright.

         How do I catch fine fat pheasants?
         Bunny rabbits too, without a gun?
         How do I make hordes of peasants
         Swear they serve my master, every one?
         Why do ogres, in my presence,
         Shrink away, turn into mice, and run?
         Come to think of it, it's dress-sense:
         Putting on the boots is how it's done.

         All you need is smooth soft leather,
         And a winning way with fancy chat.
         On your head a jaunty feather
         Sprouting from a most imposing hat.
         When you get all these together
         Nothing can stop you - if you're a cat.
         All the same, I'm doubtful whether
         Anything like this needs tricks like that.

MUSIC ENDS.

CINDERS: But Puss, you're supposed to be terribly clever.

PUSS: Well, yes. I can normally manage, whatever.
But, no Santa Claus - why, it's so unbelievable,
I can't come up with a scheme that's conceivable.
None of my cunning can be any use
Without Father Christmas.

ALADDIN: Well, here's Mother Goose.
Oh dear, and she's gone into one of her flaps.
Hey, Robin, help grab her. She's going to collapse.

ALADDIN AND ROBIN RUSH TO SUPPORT MOTHER GOOSE, WHO ENTERS
DISTRAUGHT, WAVING SMELLING-SALTS, FAN, AND HANDKERCHIEF.

GOOSE: Now come on, where is he? I can't take the strain.
I'm all of a flutter, and fainting again.

CINDERS RUSHES TO ADMINISTER SMELLING-SALTS.

GOOSE: (RECOVERING SLIGHTLY)
This wig you know, Darlings. It's too hot by half.
And then there's my corset. Please! Nobody laugh -
I'll have to have words with my dressing-room staff.
I like being tight, and the girl went to town
To get me squeezed into this wonderful gown -
But now SOMETHING tells me it's on upside-down.

ALADDIN, ROBIN, CINDERS AND PUSS SUPPRESS GIGGLES.

GOOSE: It's no joke! The agony's simply fantastic!
It's whalebone, you see. Not a hint of elastic.
If I don't go on soon, I'll do something drastic.

CINDERS: Oh, dear Mother Goose, we do please beg you not to.

GOOSE: Then YOU tell me where Father Christmas has got to.

ROBIN: Well, nobody's seen him. If only they had.

GOOSE: Then somebody FIND him, before I go mad.

RUDOLPH DESPERATELY TRIES TO SEMAPHORE WITH HIS NOSE, AND GESTURE,
BUT THE GOODIES ONLY PAT HIM AND TAKE NO NOTICE.

GOOSE: My make-up's already beginning to cake.
With thin skin like mine that's a big risk to take.
One's Art, of course Darlings, makes one SUCH a martyr -
But these heels are KILLING me. So is this garter.
(STARTS PULLING UP PETTICOATS)

GOODIES ARE EMBARRSSED.

ALADDIN: Yes, well, Santa's late. So, something's delayed him.
I think we should all attempt something to aid him.

GOODIES GATHER FOR A CONFERENCE.

RUDOLPH: (TO AUDIENCE)
       Lighting a bonfire would be the most sensible.
       Why must my signals be incomprehensible?

ROBIN: Right then, we'll load all the toys on the sleigh,
       Ready for Rudolph to tow them away.

RUDOLPH: (TO AUDIENCE)
       At last! Now they'll follow, as I lead them round,
       To show them where Santa's in icicles bound.

ALADDIN: Yes, that seems to be the most useful idea.
       We'll each get a toy, and assemble them here.

CINDERS: Ooh, bags I that big cuddly brown teddy bear.

ALADDIN: I fancy that doll, with the long golden hair.

PUSS: And I like the look of this "Ace Astronaut".
       Come on, Mother Goose. Do stop looking distraught.

GOOSE: I'm not humping toys about - highly improper.
       Although I COULD take to this old-fashioned copper.

ROBIN: Just look at this nurse. Oh, how perfectly sweet!
       She's got every last tiny detail complete.
       We never had such toys when I was a girl.

ALADDIN: Then let's make the most of them. Give them a whirl.

GOODIES START LIFTING TOYS, TALKING TO THEM, EXAMINING THEM.

RUDOLPH: Oh, this is hopeless. Now they want to play.
       Why can't they follow me towards the sleigh?
       They're so besotted with the toys they've chosen
       They'll NEVER find out Santa Claus is frozen.

MUSIC 15: "SHEPHERDS SHAKE OFF YOUR DROWSY SLEEP"

GOODIES: Come along, Toys, and let us see
       How exciting you can be.
       Now you can sit no longer lurking,
       We must make sure that you're properly working.
       Come on, let's see you stand alone.
       Now, try walking on your own.

TOYS START MOVING JERKILY. MUSIC CONTINUES.

GOODIES: Wonderful, Toys. Now here's your chance:
       Listen to the music and dance.
       Goodness! You do look realistic -
       Making each move individualistic.
       Fabulous toys to be among!
       Far advanced from when we were young.

MUSIC CONTINUES AS TOYS AND GOODIES DANCE.

TOYS' DANCE. THIS CAN BE A SIMPLE FOLK DANCE, OR IMPROVISATIONS
BASED ON THE CHARACTERS, OR A SPECTACULAR DISPLAY WITH ACROBAT
NATIONAL DANCES, BALLET, JAZZ, POP, AND APPROPRIATE PARTY PIECES -
WHATEVER SUITS THE TOYS (AND GOODIES) AVAILABLE.
OTHER MUSIC CAN BE INSERTED AS DESIRED.
AS THE MUSIC ENDS, THE CHIMES LEADING TO MIDNIGHT START.
GOODIES FREEZE AND TOYS RESUME THEIR MOTIONLESS POSITIONS,
SCATTERED OVER THE FLOOR.

MUSIC 16: "JINGLE BELLS" - very slowly

GOODIES: Christmas bells, Christmas bells,
We can hear them chime.
Midnight's come. Santa Claus
Will never be on time.
Oh
Stop it bells, stop it bells,
Please make some delay.
If Father Christmas doesn't come,
There'll be no Christmas Day.

MUSIC ENDS.

PUSS: I hate to issue tiding unfelicitous,
But I espy some most unwelcome visitors.

QUEEN AND BADDIES ENTER, TO SURVEY SAD GOODIES
AND COLLAPSED TOYS.

QUEEN: We heard a highly jolly hullabaloo,
And wondered what the world was coming to.
Though now you look a pretty sorry crew.

CINDERS: Oh, please. Where's Santa Claus? Is he with you?

QUEEN: Well. Yes, and no. Perhaps it's time you knew.

MUSIC 17: "LONDON'S BURNING"

BADDIES: Father Christmas isn't coming
We've frozen him solid
Ha ha, ha ha,
Aren't we horrid? Aren't we horrid?

GOODIES: Father Christmas not coming?
You've frozen him solid?
No no, no no,
You are horrid. You are horrid.

AND THEY SING IN EIGHT-PART CANON

BADDIES: No Christmas is coming
We'll freeze you all solid.
Ha ha, ha ha,
Aren't we horrid? Aren't we horrid?

GOODIES: No Christmas is coming.
They're freezing us solid!
Oh no, oh no,
This is horrid. This is horrid.

BY THE FADING OF THE LAST LINE OF THE CANON, THE GOODIES ARE
FROZEN INTO A TABLEAU. BADDIES CONGRATULATE EACH OTHER AND
START DESTROYING DECORATIONS AND SUBSTITUTING ICICLES UNDER
QUEEN'S DIRECTION. THEY SHOULD MOVE IN SLOW MOTION.

MUSIC 18: "LULLAY THOU LITTLE TINY CHILD"

RUDOLPH: Many's the time I've idly thought
Christmas was just a chore:
The frantic dashing round distraught -
Oh, it seemed such a bore.

But when I think of dying fires,
Stockings that won't be filled,
Of unlit candles, silent choirs,
Oh, then my heart is chilled.

Crackers, and hats, and lights that glow,
Carols and Christmas trees,
And brandy butter, mistletoe -
How can we lose all these?

Family games, and children's fun
Vanish and fade away.
If only I could find someone
Who can save Christmas Day.

MUSIC ENDS.

RUDOLPH: (TO AUDIENCE)
Oh dear, look at Robin, and poor Mother Goose.
All frozen like that they're a fat lot of use.
But the Snow Queen's so full of her icicle-spree
She still hasn't bothered to start freezing me.
So I must save Christmas. But what can I do?
If I make a move, then she'll freeze me up too.

The only way out will be one that employs
The fact that the Snow Queen can't freeze up the Toys.
But they'll never move on their own - unless YOU
Could move them - But no. Then she'd freeze you up too.
It seems an impossible situation.
UNLESS ... you could use your IMAGINATION.

Each one pick a Toy, and imagine it lives.
Make it move, with the strength your imagining gives.
Come on, everybody.

TOYS TWITCH, AND COLLAPSE

RUDOLPH: You've got it. Well ... nearly.

Let's try it again.

TOYS TWITCH, AND COLLAPSE.

RUDOLPH: Are you ALL trying? REALLY?
I'm sure you can do it. Supposing you thought
About just one Toy. Try the Ace Astronaut.
Now, concentrate. Yes. And you're going to achieve it.
He's moving! And all because you can believe it.

MUSIC 19: "GOOD KING WENCESLAS"

SPACE: What a space-walk! What a dance!
I was into orbit.
Though I never got the chance
Really to absorb it.

There I was, just back from Mars,
Party hardly started,
When again I'm seeing stars -
All the fun departed.
(INSPECTS COLLAPSED TOYS)

Now, these bodies on the floor
Make me feel a new fear.
Alien invaders, or
Some plague has been through here.

Such attacks I can survive,
In a space-suit so good.
(NOTICES BADDIES MOVING)
But those creatures, still alive,
Must be up to no good.

(POINTS CALCULATOR AT BADDIES)
Monsters, I am reading you
You're inhuman raiders.
It's my duty to subdue
All robot invaders.

I don't care what arms you've brought
From what far-away sun.
No android or cybernaut
Can withstand this ray-gun.

MUSIC ENDS. SPACE POINTS GUN. BADDIES LAUGH. QUEEN LOOMS.

QUEEN: What a ridiculous little song.
Back in your box, where you belong.
And don't go calling ME a machine!
That's what YOU are. I am a Queen.

SPACE: Are you? I'd never have realised.
(INDICATES FROZEN GOODIES)
Why are these people immobilised?

3 verses

Why are those hideous creatures here?
(POINTS CALCULATOR AT BADDIES)
Why is there such a bad atmosphere?
(POINTS CALCULATOR AT HER)
If you're a Queen, then why, for a start,
Doesn't my meter detect your heart?

QUEEN: Oh, do run along. You're too absurd.
Little toys should be seen, not heard.

SPACE BLASTS HER WITH RAY-GUN, BUT TO NO EFFECT. QUEEN LAUGHS
NASTILY AND RETURNS TO BADDIES, WHO CONTINUE WRECKING SCENERY.

SPACE: (INTO CALCULATOR)
Ace Space Man to Ground Control.
Beam up help; I'm in a hole.

RUDOLPH: (TO AUDIENCE)
Come on then. Your power's improving.
Get the Nurse and Copper moving.
Ready, steady, all believe
And ... yes ... it's working. Keep on ... heave.

NURSE AND COPPER EVENTUALLY RISE AND JOIN SPACEMAN.

MUSIC 20: "GOOD KING WENCESLAS"

COPPER: Evening, sir, and evening all.
Are we having trouble?

NURSE: I just got an urgent call.
Came here at the double.

SPACE: Glad you both beamed up so fast.
Seems we've been invaded.
Even with my laser blast
I can't cope unaided.

BADDIES ARE RIPPING DECORATIONS AND PRANCING WILDLY -
STILL IN GROTESQUE SLOW MOTION. MUSIC CONTINUES.

NURSE: Looks like mass insanity.
They need psycho-testing.

COPPER: Shocking vandals. Seems to me
They just want arresting.
(STROLLS TO BADDIES, LOOKING IMPORTANT)

All right, you lot. I'm the Law.
No point looking bitter.
I shall have to book you, for ...
(INDICATES TORN DECORATIONS STREWN AROUND)
Dropping all this litter.

MUSIC ENDS. BADDIES GATHER ROUND COPPER, NURSE AND SPACE
IN MOCKING DISBELIEF.

QUEEN: Now that's enough, you silly toys.
            Go away and stop your noise.
            There's no place or time to play -
            We've abolished Christmas Day.

BADDIES GRUNT AND CHEER APPROVAL. COPPER IS UNDETERRED.

COPPER: 'Scuse me, madam. Pardon me.
            Got to do my job, you see.
            Of the Law I am the warder -
            Got to maintain peace and order.
            (TAKES OUT NOTEBOOK)
            Now then, let me get this right.
            You maintain that Christmas Night
            Doesn't lead to Christmas Morning?

QUEEN AND BADDIES NOD AND GRIN.

COPPER: I shall have to give you warning.
            Anti-social acts like this
            Interferes with people's bliss.
            (WALKS ROUND GOODIES, INSPECTING THEM)
            Furthermore, I see you've chosen
            Certain Goodies to have frozen.
            (FROWNS AND SHAKES HIS HEAD)
            Can't have that, now can we, madam?

QUEEN SURVEYS OUTRAGED BADDIES, LONGING TO ATTACK TOYS.

QUEEN: All right, Baddies. Up and at 'em.

GIANT: Smack them till they crack in bits.

SILVER: Crush them till their stuffing splits.

SCROOGE: Loose their screws and cut their strings.

UGLIES: Rip out all their wheels and springs.

BADDIES MENACE THE THREE TOYS, WHO ARE TOO QUICK FOR THEM.

MUSIC 21: "GOOD KING WENCESLAS"

NURSE: Baddies, you are out of date.
            We are not clockwork. It's
            Silicon, and solid state,
            And computer circuits.

            Seems it's time that you were told
            Science is fantstic.,
            We're all super, seamless-mould
            Polyprop'lene plastic.

1 Verse

THEY ATTACK THE BADDIES WITH RAY-GUN, TRUNCHEON AND
HYPODERMIC, DOING FAIRLY WELL, BUT NOT WELL ENOUGH.

RUDOLPH:(TO AUDIENCE)
        Boys and girls, it's up to you.
        Make believe, and bring them through.

MUSIC 22: "O TANNENBAUM"/THE RED FLAG

SPACE)   Come all you toys, and fight the foe.
COPPER: We CAN save Christmas Night, you know.
NURSE)   We may be small, but we are strong.
        And we are right, while they are wrong.

        So come and have a smashing time
        To stamp out bad and conquer crime.
        Just join the Space Force, and Police,
        And Red Cross, till they beg for peace.

TEDDY, DOLL AND OTHER TOYS RISE AND JOIN THE FIGHT, MOVING
JERKILY, DOING THE ACTIONS THEY SING. BADDIES ACCOMPANY
"THUD" WITH "OUCH" EACH TIME A TOY HITS, KICKS OR PRODS.

TOYS: The goodies may be frozen quite (THUD)
        But we are warm and free tonight (THUD)
        We'll twist your arms and squash your toes (THUD)
        And pull your hair, and tweak your nose (THUD)

        We'll give you cause (THUD) to grunt and groan (THUD)
        And leave the Snow (THUD) Queen on her own (THUD)
        She's icy cold (THUD) but never fear (THUD)
        We'll warm up Winter once a year. (FINAL THUD)

QUEEN: How very clever. If I didn't hate you
        I almost feel I would congratulate you.

TOYS   Unfreeze the Goodies! Unfreeze Santa Claus!
        And give us Christmas back. It isn't yours.

QUEEN: Oh, I'm afraid it is, my dears. You see
        There's nothing you can do to unfreeze ME.
        No ordinary fire could even start
        To melt the block of ice which is my heart
        No fire could be so hot, and yet so small.
        And so, you see, you have no hope at all.

RUDOLPH:(SHOUTING TO TOYS)
        I have it. I've a fire which hotly glows.
        A tiny ball. Quick, someone, take my nose.

A TOY REMOVES HIS NOSE AND HOLDS IT TO THE COWERING QUEEN.

MUSIC 23: "I SAW THREE SHIPS"

TOYS: We see a way to melt you now
        On Christmas Day, on Christmas Day.
        For good old Rudolph showed us how
        On Christmas Day in the morning.

       You can't pretend it's really nice,
       On Christmas Day, on Christmas Day,
       To have a heart that's made of ice,
       On Christmas Day in the morning.

MUSIC SLOWS

QUEEN: My melting heart, it makes me weep
           On Christmas Day, on Christmas Day.
           All right, your Christmas you can keep!

TOYS: Hip hip hooray in the morning.

           And as your heart with pity thaws
           On Christmas Day, on Christmas Day,
           Unfreeze the Goodies and Santa Claus
           On Christmas Day in the morning.

QUEEN: I melt the spell, I set them free,
           On Christmas Day, on Christmas Day.
           You modern toys are too much for me
           On Christmas Day in the morning.

MUSIC ENDS. GOODIES STRETCH STIFFLY AND CONFRONT
REVIVING BADDIES.

SANTA BUSTLES IN, BRUSHING SNOW AND ICICLES FROM ALL OVER HIM.

SANTA: I must have dozed off. Dreamt I had a tiff
          With all the Baddies. Woke up frozen stiff.
          (SEES BADDIES AND GOODIES STANDING AROUND)
          Well, don't just stand there. What are you DOING here?
          You should be off-stage, waiting to appear.
          And who's been interfering with the toys?
          It really is too much. I'm most annoyed.
          (NOTICES RUDOLPH'S NOSE IS MISSING)
          Now who's done this? Why's Rudolph's nose been taken?
          It's CHRISTMAS everybody! Get your skates on!

A TOY REPLACES RUDOLPH'S NOSE. QUEEN APPROACHES SANTA.

QUEEN: So sorry, Father Christmas. All my fault.
          I wanted to bring Christmas to a halt.

SANTA: I DIDN'T dream it then.
          (FLEXES MUSCLES AND CALMS DOWN)
                   Still, no harm done.
          Let's all get on with Christmas, everyone.
          (SHOOS PEOPLE AROUND)

SILVER: Not ALL of us. Just count me out for one.

SCROOGE: Count me out too.

GIANT: .   Me three.

SANTA: But ... it's such fun.

GIANT: You keep on saying that. I don't agree.
           So ... count me out ... as four.

UGLY 1:   And me.

UGLY 2:   And me.

SANTA: For goodness' sake, please, have your wits about you.
           There can't be any pantomimes without you.

BADDIES: For badness' sake, we're glad there won't be any.
           The Goodies get their way in far too many.

SANTA CONTINUES TRYING TO PERSUADE THEM, BUT UNSUCCESSFULLY.

RUDOLPH: (TO AUDIENCE)
           Persuasion won't do any good, I fear.
           What HE needs is a really bright idea.
           A flash of inspiration. Well, here goes.
           The brightest thing around here is my nose.

RUDOLPH MOVES TO SANTA, FLASHING NOSE. LIGHT DAWNS.

SANTA: (TO BADDIES)
           I've got it! A way
           To make you desist.
           When I've had my say
           You'll never persist.
           You'll have to obey -
           You cannot resist.
           I'm sure you will stay,
           And be glad to get hissed.

BADDIES SHAKE HEADS.

SANTA: You DON'T want to play?
           Well, if you insist.
           Depart as you may
           BUT, think about this:
           The very first day
           That a panto is missed,
           The price you will pay
           Is: YOU CEASE TO EXIST!

GIANT: Er ... what does that mean?

SCROOGE: It means WE have to die.

SILVER: It means we're all scuppered.

GIANT: But ... I don't see why.

UGLY 1:   You wouldn't.

UGLY 2:   You're stupid.

GIANT: That's not very nice

QUEEN: Stop arguing, all of you. Hear my advice.
What Santa Claus tells you is perfectly true.
If pantomimes end, it's the end of you.

UGLY 1: Well, that is the limit!

UGLY 2:   I don't want to die!

QUEEN: I think that your anger had best be put by,
At least for the moment. Save up all your rage
And then let it out on a pantomime stage.

BADDIES: We'll rant and we'll rave. We'll be perfectly rotten.

GOODIES: That's great. And your treachery won't be forgotten.

RELIEVED, SANTA STARTS LOADING SLEIGH WHICH RUDOLPH BRINGS.

GOODIES, TOYS, AND EVENTUALLY BADDIES SING - SOLOS AND
CHORUS AS DESIRED.

MUSIC 24: "MORNING HAS BROKEN"

ALL   Morning is breaking,
            Christmas Day dawning.
            We must be making
            Way through the snow.
            Thanks to the children,
            Thanks to the baby
            Born in a manger
            Ages ago.

            Brightly the snow lies,
            White as a blanket,
            Wrapping the world up
            Cosy and warm.
            As we remember
            The heavenly stranger,
            Visiting Earth that
            First Christmas morn.

            Soon there'll be sleigh bells,
            Mingled with church bells.
            Soon there'll be hymns and
            Carols to sing.
            Heavenly peace, and
            Earthly enjoyment,
            Presents and blessings
            Christmas will bring.

            Farewell today, and
            Prosper tomorrow.
            May you be free from
            Sorrow and fear.
            Our entertainment
            Draws to its ending.

So, Merry Christmas,
Happy New Year.

THE SLEIGH IS LADEN WITH TOYS. RUDOLPH IS HARNESSED AND
DRAWS IT OFF. GOODIES WAVE TO SLEIGH PASSING OVERHEAD.

MUSIC 25: "JINGLE BELLS"

GOODIES: Jingle bells, Jingle Bells,
Jingle all the way.
Oh what fun it is to wave
At Santa Claus's sleigh
OH
Jingle bells, jingle bells,
Rudolph leads the way,
Guiding all the toys at last
On Santa Claus's sleigh.

Dashing through the sky
On a reindeer-driven sleigh.
Through the stars they fly,
Shining all the way.
Rudolph's nose again
Saved our Christmas Night.
How funny, but how fortunate
He has a nose so bright!
OH

RUDOLPH, SANTA AND TOYS CAN RETURN FOR FINALE, AND BADDIES
CAN JOIN IN, THROWING STREAMERS THIS TIME.

ALL: Jingle bells, jingle bells,
Jingle all the way.
Oh what fun it is to star
In a happy Christmas play,
OH
Jingle bells, jingle bells,
What a jolly time.
And we hope you've all enjoyed
The ALL STAR PANTOMIME.

CURTAIN

MUSICAL NUMBERS

1 QUEEN: HARK TO ME (Hark the Herald Angels Sing)
2 QUEEN & BADDIES: O COME, ALL YOU BADDIES (O Come All Ye Faithful)
3 GIANT: ONCE I WAS A HAPPY GIANT (Once in Royal David's City)
4 SILVER: IT CAME UPON ME (It Came Upon the Midnight Clear)
5 SCROOGE: THE FIRST OF THE GHOSTS (The First Nowell)
6 UGLIES: TWO ENCHANTING SISTERS (We Three Kings)
7 BADDIES: SO ROT YOUR MERRY (God Rest You Merry, Gentlemen)
8 QUEEN: IN THE BLEAK MIDWINTER (In the Bleak Midwinter)
9 BADDIES: WE WISH YOU A HORRID (We Wish You a Merry Christmas)
10 RUDOLPH: RED-EYED REINDEER (What Child is This/Greensleeves)

11 CINDERS: ON CHRISTMAS NIGHT (On Christmas Night All Christians Sing)
12 ALADDIN: AS WITH GLADNESS (As With Gladness Men of Old)
13 ROBIN: ZING BONG (Ding Dong Merrily + Angels from the Realms of Glory)
14 PUSS: LET ME NOW (Deck the Hall with Boughs of Holly)
15 GOODIES: COME ALONG TOYS (Shepherds Shake Off Your Drowsy Sleep)
  TOYS: OPTIONAL EXTRA SONG AND DANCE NUMBERS
16 GOODIES: CHRISTMAS BELLS (Jingle Bells)
17 BADDIES & GOODIES: FATHER CHRISTMAS CANON (London's Burning)
18 RUDOLPH: MANY'S THE TIME (Lullay Thou Little Tiny Child)
19 SPACE: WHAT A SPACE-WALK (Good King Wenceslas)
20 COPPER, NURSE & SPACE: EVENING SIR AND EVENING ALL (Good King Wenceslas)
21 NURSE: BADDIES, YOU ARE OUT OF DATE (Good King Wenceslas)
22 TOYS: COME ALL YOU TOYS (O Tannenburg/The Red Flag)
23 TOYS: WE SEE A WAY (I Saw Three Ships)
24 COMPANY: MORNING IS BREAKING (Morning Has Broken)
25 COMPANY: JINGLE BELLS (Jingle Bells)

PRODUCTION NOTES

STYLE OF PERFORMANCE

Each performer should dominate the stage and audience for his or her solo pieces and remain unobtrusively in character at other times. Since much of the spectacle consists of sitting or standing figures, actors need to develop distinctive poses which they can hold. Movements and speech should be broad and stylised, with everything larger than life. Rhyme and metre make the lines easy to learn, but they need to be fully acted and not rushed, to bring out not only the menace, emotion and suspense, but also the surprises and humour.

REHEARSING

The show is intentionally easy to prepare: each solo or chorus routine can be worked out separately and only the last two numbers require a full cast. This means that a good deal of rehearsing can be done in small groups or by individuals. It is as well for a Stage Manager to make plans of the basic tableaux for reference; a choreographer can hewith the Toys' Dance and solo routines; and although most of the action is self-explanatory a director can judge what is most effective from the audience's point of view. Since Rudolph is on stage permanently he can also direct. Most rehearsals will require an accompanist.

MUSIC

This is readily available in carol and hymn books, but may need transposing to suit the voices. If in difficulty fitting words to a tune, try singing more than one syllable per note. Much of the story is in the songs, so they need careful, characterful singing, with occasional pauses. Although a piano is adequate basic accompaniment, a selection of instruments (guitar, flute, recorder, glockenspiel, drum) can lend variety of texture and add to the atmosphere.

CASTING

Fourteen solo singers - six male - are needed. There are also two non-singing male parts (Santa and Goose) and two non-speaking children's parts (Doll, Teddy). It is a good idea to start with more than the minimum eighteen, since colds and unforeseen problems often strike. Casting extra Goodies, Baddies and Toys not only provides understudies but also enables those with little rehearsal time available to join in. Any number of children can be Toys, limited only by stage-space. The TOYS' DANCE is an opportunity to include dancers, acrobats and party-pieces if desired.

COSTUME AND MAKE-UP

Traditional costumes may be hired, but ingenious adaptation can be effective and fun. Unless you use powerful theatrical lighting, or perform in a very large hall, only simple make-up is needed.

LIGHTING

> There is scope for spectacular effects: snow, stars, mist, wind, clouds - but in a small hall the most useful equipment is a moveable spotlight with different coloured gelatines. If possible, have some fairy lights on stage in Act Two.

SETTINGS

> Vital set requirements are: snow and a moveable sleigh in Act One; destroyable decorations and hangable icicles in Act Two. Velcro is useful for these last two - fixing easily and tearing loudly. A curtain to conceal the setting of Act Two during the Interlude is valuable; so are a raised section and an apron, or steps, to enable Rudolph to be near the audience. Suggested additions: an old-fashioned proscenium arch frame; a North Pole and bleak landscape for Act One; a twinkling cave, Christmas Tree, large inanimate toys, and packing boxes for Act Two.

PROPERTIES

> Rudolph - detachable flashing nose (clown's); Silver - crutch, telescope, stuffed parrot on shoulder; Scrooge - lantern; Ugly 1 - hip-flask; Goose - smelling salts; Space - ray-gun, pocket calculator; Copper - truncheon; Nurse - hypodermic (icing-tube). Suggested additions: glitter, bubbles, balloons, snow-flakes.